BRILLIANT CORNERS

BRILLIANT CORNERS

Jeanne Heuving

chax 2022
TUCSON ARIZONA

ISBN 978-1-946104-38-0

Chax Press
1517 N Wilmot Rd no. 264
Tucson Arizona 85712-4410

Chax Press books are supported in part by individual donors and by sales of books.
Please visit https://chax.org/membership-support/ if you would like to contribute to our
mission to make an impact on the literature and culture of our time.

Writing about music is like dancing about architecture.

— Thelonious Monk

I like to do quilts of strings and pieces because I can use all the little and big pieces. I hardly ever buy material . . . .That's not what quilting is all about. Scrap quilts are the prettiest quilts.

— Nora Ezell

1

To begin with sea. I see the sea, glassy and languid, darkening and lightening in up-

swellings of blue-green, suddenly black, catching the reflection of trees. I am out to sea

with so many days yet ahead of me to stay in this cottage and to watch the lifting and

falling waters. In the presence of strong winds, the sea forms asymmetric steep crests

and broad troughs, and the choppy water is no longer reflective; this condition is known

as sea. Persistent wave movement after the wind has dropped and the mirroring revives;

this is known as swell. Citation functions as a go between personages and historical epochs. It summons words as nominations and wrenches these from their context, and

thereby calls them back to their origin. Through citation a secret meeting takes place

between past generations and the present, one book and another. As the salt water rises

and seeps into the grass and then quickly covers the depressed land, it makes inky pools

of green combed in one direction with few entanglements. Almost a true level between

land and high tide makes for a rich sea marsh, lower by a foot or so, nothing but inks

grass growing on it. Inland seas, bounded by land, are staggered at various altitudes, remnants of vaster waterways, now mere puddles and cracked declensions

amidst seas of sand, dirt and rock. It is called the Dead Sea because the

water moveth not, neither can any fishe live there. So in this windie Sea of

Land, the Fiend Walk'd up and down alone. And thou, Ione, shalt chaunt

fragments of sea-music. Over the globe is one vast Sea. In ancient times

rather than Seas surrounding the globe an immense river was thought to

encompass it.

2

To begin with ocean. I try to reach the island barren and rocky on one side and covered

with fir trees on the other but even at low tide it is stranded by ocean. The entrance into

the mouth of the river is impossible since the ocean goeth so high. It is most thrilling

rownyge just beyond the surf, and launching a barke upon the shore. O'er the ocean

swell, Sublime of Hope, I seek the cottag'd dell. Dante's Rime has no Homeric ocean roll.

Does he not resist the ocean swell within him? Ensconced in his poetic dwelling, winds

sweeping up the rocky steep, the eagle is soughed on his perch. Near the lee point, the tides with their salty residue blacken a host of stumps. Because freshwater is less dense than

saltwater, more water flows out into the ocean than backward into the watershed. Further

inland, an ocean of rolling sand dunes with tufts of grass and shadowed troughs gives way

to a flattened terrain of terse vegetation, thorny tendrils crossing uncertain paths. At the far

reaches is a grove of stunted pine trees through which the barely discernable roar of the

ocean catches on brambles. There are now too many ocean-going vessels to count, each

wedding-cake cruise liner with its multiple arcades, restaurants and swimming pools, turquoise lozenges amidst the blue ocean, alight with sun. The Flatiron building is

like the bow of a monster ocean steamer. An ocean lane is a flatted path across the

ocean, designated primarily for steamers. The great continental sag sinks below the

ocean level. The Sun hovers o're the Ocean brim. The ocean waues darken. I heard the

shadows scrying and gave them your name.

3

To begin with shore. I step onto an expanse of glistening sand, seagulls crying, reeling,

opening into sky, horizon. Next, a rocky shelf with seaweed awash at the shore and sea

grass rooted in sandy pockets. I am shorn of my usual habits as I shear a path close to the

incoming waters. Fossil evidence suggests that land plants came about through a symbiosis

of sea fungi and photosynthesizing algae, leaving their marine environment to grow upon

land. How and why some seed plants returned to the ocean is hard to say. They open their

flowers underwater, blowsy and gauzy amidst saltwater conditions. Their pollen is water born and their seeds are carried away into fertile shallows and fallows deep. Sea lions

and otters made a similar return to the habitat from which their predecessors originated,

swimming for long periods underwater and resting on rocky abutments. These reverse

directions are mysterious, although likely caused by retreat from overly crowded lands for

the greater freedom of the ocean. A shore is a piece of timber or iron set obliquely against

a building in danger of collapsing or a ship in dock undergoing alteration or repair. The

shore zone is the zone affected by wave action. When the water does not ebb or flow, there is no shore. A richness of colors, of greens turned inkish in the incoming waters and of brown kelp aswirl in an ocean of blue-brown, has no end in sight. The color line is a scrim of fact. It is not of this world, has no soul and cannot inhere in a human being.

4

To begin with landscape. I have never been so hemmed in, so turned out, than in this

quilting of fields and sea, buildings and street. In Cityscape, buildings mount on one side of

the picture plane, trapezoids and lozenges. The street narrowing in perspectival semblance

gainsays more than half way up the canvas beside angled fields pushing against its straight

edge. Abruptly, a road, a tough rut of gray, dead ends at a strip of blue. Following this line

of ascent, I am catapulted into the ocean. Here, the furthest away, buildings, trees and

bushes are the most realistic, although on closer inspection are mere dashes of paint. A slur of paint makes for a pole in a golf course, although it could be almost anything. Gray

transparent shadows, painted over opaque blocks of colors, lay on the road and land. I

began to feel that what I was really up to in painting, what I enjoyed almost exclusively,

was altering—changing what was before me. I looked forward with relief to being able

to correct, to set things right, and it was with something akin to guilt that I did so in the

privacy of my studio. Somewhat later, I realized that the arts of painting, writing and

composing music were intrinsically activities that partake of revision and that it is probably the exception for it not to be true. I like to feel that I am involved at any stage of the painting with all of its movements, not just a "now" moment where a superficial grace is available. I felt that what was becoming my painting was a wholesale proposition and that my initial intent as well as my intent in the process of realizing it was reduced to simply making things right.

5

To begin with Seawall. It lifts into the sky, shoving out ocean and air, beach and field. This

thrusting white, tan and flesh colored strip pushes back black triangles and variegated

green and yellow fields dashed with orange and noses the blue. There is an alternating

smoothness and roughness of brushwork, ending in swirled paint, an exuberance of blue

strokes, some curved, some flat, with traces of orange, red and yellow, perhaps a cloud

formation. Above to the far left of the canvas, there is more assuredly a blue cloud. The

tempest of paint and sea wall pressed against the adjacent fields bespeaks the rising heat of land masses drenched with sun. Black parallelograms and triangles stagger a diagonal, all converging at the nudging sea wall, a sea lion roaring on a rock. A horizon line shores the canvas, ends the ocean, starts the sky. Human action, if any human action at all, is as hieroglyphic marks and ink spillage, perhaps a construction crew and equipment, a conglomeration of automobiles, motorcycles and beachgoers. It is as if an earthquake has taken place, while the muted blue of the ocean sleeps on, all activity, all violence given over to land and construction. I want a painting to be difficult to do. My freedom consists in my moving about within the narrow frame that I have assigned myself for each one of my undertakings. My freedom is so much the greater and more meaningful, the more narrowly I limit my field of action and the more I surround myself with obstacles. The passion for obstacles is a defense against the end of possibilities, against the end of desire.

6

To begin with Ocean Park. I scavenge the canvas for the build up of Ocean Park, its quasi

industrial buildings, narrow roads without sidewalks, boulevards with perfectly manicured

lawns and blue ocean. I dive headlong into the blue and resurface amidst horizontal and

diagonal lines incising the picture plane and floating over it. Everything is on the surface yet

implies overlapping planes. Right angularity is freely introduced into diagonal matrices and

vice versa. Sheets of atmospheric color, drenched in mood, are flattened into pure desire.

Lines that appear to be drawn with a ruler and those that are free hand seduce us into the bright colors that speak of shadows. Lines made with graphite pencil bring

attention to edges. Inked lines manifest the desire to have the record of all the marks, the

pentimenti retained. It is not surprising that the painter turns next to paper and gouache, the

wet uneven paper shrunken with dried paint. Then, to paper cut outs, adding paper strips

to the top and bottom of his compositions, and to cigar box tops, their insignia ghosting the

overlaid paint, special gifts for friends. Finally it is heraldic signs, a black of clubs turning

into a spade, offsetting and mirroring a tree. I discovered that symbols had for me a much greater emotional charge than I realized. There is an effect of instantaneity

that the symbol provides, a forgetting of what went before. The more that is given

over to the symbol, the greater is the possibility for a dynamic between concealing

and revealing. To revise is to forget the burden of the inexact or painful memory and

replace it with the pleasure of creation. It is a totalizing gesture which negates itself.

7

To begin with medallion. I medallion my writing with the words of others. A medallion

inscribes the heraldry of ancestors on metal, cloth or paper. In this work clothes quilt

with a center medallion of corduroy, strips of faded and stretched denim from bending

knees and elbows and polyester blues and browns frame the center block. On the right,

double stitched denim seams with additional marking from the doubled over cloth hold

in abeyance the strips on the left where darker blues prevail. Two small patches patch the

bands above and beneath the centerpiece. Everything else is in strips, including a small barely visible band of black and white checkered cloth, on two sides only, and then only

partially on one. The medallion is gold, umber and vermillion corduroy, pieced into the

predominantly indigo field of impervious and worn threads, a mango slashed from stem

to navel, a papaya with gooey black seeds. Work clothes are commemorative of those

working in the fields and other farm jobs, and corduroy strips with their ridges and troughs

replicate the enduring strip composition. Strip design originated with narrow looms and

were transmitted from the Mande to the Kongo peoples and eventually to the new world in quilt design among other textile practices. While African languages that

crossed the Atlantic were systematically destroyed, aesthetic preferences and their

cultural reach were transmitted visually and aurally. I have to find a way to do it

myself. When I sit down, I got to get into a mind of my own. My daddy plowed fields

in those overalls and I chopped cotton in this dress.

8

To begin with medallion. In this housetop with a center medallion, intermittent patches of cut-off flora and fauna make for a pleasing enigma. Two triangles, constituting the only diagonals, mark an off-center center, squared by two bands and borders inset by borders. I think to have found the outer most border that becomes through color adjacency another border, so while there is an overall impression of interlocking squares, they transform into multiple pathways going round and round. Patches of dashinki cloth make for additional borders within borders, and repetitive machine patterns of diamonds and polk-a-dot stay attention on individual patches. The pine green, pinkish salmons, and pastel pinks are emboldened by black squares that may signify panther spots or prayer. A single strip of cloth depicting stylized plant-life calms the action on the far right. There is no sense of a controlling geometry as color melds with patterning and patterning melds with color. Small irregularities settle and unsettle this balanced and whimsical composition. I got an old dress. I hold that dress up. Get my scissors and cut it. Jeans, I just tear them loose. When I start to piecing my quilts I get all of my pieces. I have them in a box right here. I got to start in my lap. I get my piece where I want to put it. And I just sew it together. I don't plan anything. I just get my pieces and then start piecing, just start sewing. I stay with what I start out, old clothes I can tear up. It always comes out level. Time now had a hole in it.

9

To begin with Gee's Bend. Gee's Bend is a cluster of black hamlets, surrounded by the

looping Alabama River and its swamps, sometimes called Alabama Africa. By the depths of

the Great Depression, Gee's Bend was as poor as any place in the United States, the price

of cotton having fallen by ninety per cent and the net worth of each person less than four

dollars. Gee's Bend was named for its first plantation owner Joseph Gee, succeeded by

Mark Pettway, owner of land and slaves, and then after the Civil War, only land, which he

rented out to black tenement farmers, until it fell into the hands of the robber barrons and bankrupt ensigns, Adrian Van De Graff and E. O. Rentz. Then came Roosevelt's New

Deal offering the possibility of land purchase and project houses. Housetop quilts with a

medallion center were and are by far the most popular form of quilts in Gee's Bend, their

squares and rectangles opening into rooms and chambers of needs and wants. The absent

signatures are many, America Irby, Ella Mae Irby, Mary Lee Bendolph, Delia Bennett,

Arie Pettway, Jessie Pettway, Loretta Pettway, Plummer Pettway, Annie May Young, Nettie

Young. The time of year the cotton opens up, we pick cotton. After you finish with the cotton you go back to quilting. I sit down and hold my hands, and I feel bad. I do my

quilt pieces and go to sewing and I feel all right. Quilts dress up the house, make it

look good. Newspapers on the walls stop up the cracks and keep out the cold. They

protect against enslaving spirits since evil spirits have to stop and read the words of

each chopped up column. I have a mind to quilt. I saw it all as from a distance, as if

thru an eye made of opera glass.

10

To begin with folding. I fold cloth, doubling it back until the entire material lies in piles,

wrapping the cloth round the end to make an envelope. I fold a quilt at the end of the

bed and press down on it, which letting go, springs into a heap on the floor. Why would

something be folded if it were not to be enveloped, wrapped or put into something else.

Inclusion or inherence has a condition of closure or envelopment, which Leibniz put

forward in his formula, "no windows." When inclusion is accomplished, it is done so

continuously and includes the sense of a finished act, however much this act must be done again and again. It is neither the site, the place, nor the point of view, and without

which, point of view would not be. It is necessarily a soul, a subject. She wore over

her great gown of stiff ticking, an apron of even stiffer material, so as not to sully her

underdress. At feast great persons were wont to change their ordinary clothes for a white

Synthesis. The chief of operations was dressed in a loose Synthesis, a dress of white twill,

unconfined by a girdle. The whole world exists only in the folds of the soul which convey

it. We think souls evanescent, transparent, but they are more like baffles. The stolidity of a soul baffles all arguments. We are baffled at sea by tempestuous weather, which

when quieted makes of the blue-gray, a tufted quilt with minimal ripple. It is possible

that two or even three distinct words are confused in baffle. Cotton waste when beaten

out soft, turned into batting, is used for baffle in coverlets. Go to the field, pick cotton.

Go to the gin, wrap it up, put wadding in the quilt.

11

To begin with charm. I am charmed by the words of others, which I change into my

words by putting pen to paper, copying and altering these as my hand moves over fibrous

textures, dying the macerated pulp blue and sometimes black, then tap on a keyboard and

watch the letters, coded into the hard drive, appear on the screen. I hit print and transfer

my words to an inkjet printer, black marks appearing on fiber. I choose charms to work

their spell on other charms, cleaving words. Kongo charms often take on the allegory of the

cosmos miniaturized. God is imagined at the top, the dead at the bottom, and waters in between. Shiny objects indicate water and can be both inside the charm and outside.

When nkisi nkita nsumbu is unwrapped, revealing its medicines, it is like looking through

clear water at the pebble-strewn bottom of a river. In prenda, Sugar cane filled with

seawater, sand and mercury is stoppered with wax, and carries the action of quicksilver

and the swift and moving waters of the ocean, so that the spirit of the charm can merge

with the sea and travel far away. In figurines, medicine can be inserted in the abdomen or

in the horn or cone, the latter corked with a piece of mirror. Mirrors conjure mystical vision. The rightful person will never be destroyed but may come back as an everlasting pool, waterfall, or rock. One might pray to a seashell. As strong as your house you will keep my life for me. When you leave for the sea, take me along, that I may live forever with you. There is a tradition of enclosing writing in charms, because of the knowledge thought to be inherent in writing. A turn in the path or the crossroads is the intersection between the ancestors and the living.

12

To begin with seawater. The small lapping wavelets keep my attention on the grayed

surface, suddenly seeing through to the magnified pebbles, their gold, black and white. The

water with its runnels is as a smoothed out cloth that has been crushed into a ball. The Ki-

Kongon verb futika or to fold also means to bind, to hold in a packet. Get a strip of cloth

about a foot long and three inches wide. Name the cloth after the absent person. Fold the

cloth three times towards yourself, so that half of it is folded saying with each fold, "Come

on home." Then turn the other end toward yourself and make three more folds.

Then stick pins through the fabric, and say the person's name and "Won't you come." The writer travels with his Inuit guide to Wakeham Bay, a two-and-a half mile wide slab of ice that heaves up and down with the tides, leaving its edges strewn with automobile-sized blocks of ice. With his *tourq,* Lukasi chops a hole in the three-foot thick ice and while the tide is still out shimmies into the hollow regions beneath the shelf of ice to forage for blue mussels. Following him, the writer is disoriented by a plunge from a bright, frigid upper world into the dark warm underworld—the temperature of the moving sea. As I adjust to the eerie surroundings, my breath shallow and quick, I feel as if I have dropped into an

entirely unknown and unexpected realm, as if the tiny hole carved by Lukasi allowed

us to slip mysteriously, not just under the ice, but beneath the surface of the sea. Here,

in a dreamlike state, I feel inside the body of the ocean. As my eyes adjust to the

dim, sultry realm below the ice, I see Lukasi, his silhouette bobbing deep in the cave,

already picking mussels. The air is thick. I taste the saltiness.

13

To begin with Epistrophy. Give your life to epistrophy, give your faith to epistrophy, raise

your hands to epistrophy. To begin the melody in the left hand and pass it over to the right,

drum it left, right. Spoil it, mischord it, open into a bigger right, left. A carry through on the

ring shout, circling counter clockwise and the marching funereal bands of New Orleans

with their drums, tubas and trumpets taken up by that percussive, string instrument, the

piano. The playing is linear but the hands are symmetrical, a symmetry doubled into four

hands when the backboard is a mirror. The name of my piece is "Opposable Thumb at the

Water's Edge." There seems to be an innate opportunism to the fact of having been born

at this point in our evolution at least, with opposable thumbs. This accounts, I think,

for overtones of manipulation—the Latin word hand, you'll remember, is *manus*—

which contend and otherwise complicate the 'innocence' of touch. Graspability is a

self-incriminating thirst native to every hand, an indigenous court from which only the

drowned hope to win acquittal. The piece makes use of two utility riffs: "whatever

beginnings go back to" and "an exegetic refusal to be done with desire." We are always amongst and between notes, on the way from note to notes, or notes to note. Our

hearing does not remain with notes, it reaches through these and beyond, and back

into what we just heard, as the just plucked forever imposes on what went before and

what comes next. When you look at the keyboard, all the notes are already there. But

if you mean a note enough, it will sound different. You got to pick the notes you really

mean. A note can be as small as a pin or as big as the world.

14

To begin with Criss Cross. I cross over a nearly submerged sand bar at the water's edge, the

incoming waters criss crossed with ripples from the mounting winds. When the current,

setting in one direction meets up with a wind going in a somewhat different direction,

there is a criss cross or rip tide. I cross my left hand over my right, and place it back on the

keyboard, two crosses hanging mid-air. Musicians are obliged to be ambidexters, some are

more ambidexters than others. Ambidexterity causes altered connections between the right

and left sides of the brain, leading to increased or decreased connectivity between language centers and somatosensory cortices. Left hemisphere lesions result in an omissive response bias or error pattern whereas right hemisphere lesions result in a commisive response bias or error pattern. Depression is linked with a hyperactive right hemisphere and relatively inactive left hemisphere, leading to selective involvement in processing negative emotions, pessimistic thoughts and unconstructive thinking as well as to vigilance, arousal and self-reflection. The Kongo cosmogram depicting a cross within an ellipsis manifest their relationship to their world, the worlds of the living and dead. Two mountain ranges mirror each other and are separated by water. The rising and

setting sun causes day and night to alternate in the two worlds. Kainga, or water, is

represented by the horizontal yewa line. I get tired of sitting down at the piano. I get

up and dance so I can dig the rhythm better. I hit the piano with my elbow because of

a certain sound I want to hear, certain chords. You can't hit that many notes with your

hands. Sometimes people laugh when I'm doing that. Yeah, let 'em laugh! They need

something to laugh at.

15

To begin with Brilliant Corners. I walk into the darkened alley way, angular sunlight

stabbing down. Steps so bold they sink into danger, so resolute they hit the pavement and

repel mud. A richness of technique that embellishes the shadows and blinds the center.

A run up and a run down. A run down and a run up. A triangular vacant lot on which

nothing has been built since it is inhospitable to rectangular houses. I gazed long into the

grassy hillock; and stooping down, perceived a hole still full of snail-shells and pebbles,

which we were fond of storing there along with more perishable things; and as fresh as reality it appeared that I beheld my early playmate seated on the withered turf: his dark,

square head bent forward, and his little hand scooping out the earth with a piece of slate.

Trinkle Tinkle trickles a variegated stream, a mountain spring that carves a listening in the

forest and groove in the granite. It turns and twists, treble and bass sounds braided and let

loose. Advance and entrance. Entrance and advance. Thirst is by its nature unquenchable.

It reminds of the hopelessness of hope and the presumptiousness of despair. What is an

original? If it sound original. It has to have its own sound. Don't play everything or every time, let some things go by. What you don't play can be more important than what

you do. You know any body can play a composition and use far out chords and make

it sound wrong. It's making it sound right that's not easy. Anything that's very good

will make you laugh in admiration, so it must humor to make you laugh—or maybe

it makes you laugh in surprise because it knocks you out. I'm after new chords, new

ways of syncopating, new figures, new runs. How to use notes differently. That's it. Just

using notes differently.

16

To begin with Introspection. Introspection casts a mentality on things calling attention to

itself. Introspection turns mental processes outwards, metals oxidizing into graduated color

sheens. The cold of mentality goes bone deep and arrests us from our usual slumbers.

Locomotive chug-a-lugs as the train steadily slows into the station at Rocky Mount. The

difficulty of climbing a rocky mountain enters as a jagged syncopation that is endlessly

arriving. Writing about music is like dancing about architecture. The intervallic leaps are as

big as a house. Do you realize what its like to be a musician and to hear his own composition and not to be able to get inside a club. Henry Minton was generous with

loans and would put a pot of food on the range for unemployed friends. But he provided

a necessity more important than food: a place in which to hold interminable jam sessions,

the "cutting session" of improvisational skill and physical endurance between two or more

musicians. After the jazzman learned the fundamentals of his instrument and the traditional

techniques of jazz—the intonations, the mute work, manipulations of timbre, the body of

traditional styles, he must "find himself," must be reborn, must discover, as it were his soul. His instructors are his fellow musicians. His recognition depends upon their

acceptance of his ability as having reached a standard. The important thing is how

he feels. How I feel don't mean nothing. He'll be the way he wants to be, the way he

supposed to be. Everyone is influenced by everybody but you bring it down home the

way you feel it. All musicians are subconsciously mathematicians.

17

To begin with Soultrane. Soultrane, successively, one car at a time, couples with Blue

Train. I'd go by Monk's house, by his apartment, and get him out of bed maybe. And then

he'd wake up and go over to the piano and start playing. He'd play anything, like one of

his tunes or whatever. He'd start playing it, and he'd look at me. I'd get my horn and start

trying to find what he's playing, and he tended to play over and over, and over and over,

and I'd get this part, and next time he'd go over it I'd get another part. And he'd stop to

show me parts that were pretty difficult, and if I had a lot of trouble, well he would get his portfolio out and show me the music. He's got music, he's got all of them written, and I'd read it and learn it. He'd rather a guy learned without reading it, because that way you feel it better. You feel it quicker when you memorize it, when you learn it by heart, by ear. And so when I almost had the tune down, then he would leave me with it. He'd leave me to practice it alone, and he'd go out somewhere, maybe he'd go to the store or back to bed or something. Finally I had it pretty well and then I'd call him and we'd play it down together. Slack action is the amount of free movement of one car before it transmits

its motion to the next car. This free movement occurs because cars are loosely

coupled and often combined with a shock-absorbing device, a draft gear, which under

stress, substantially increases the free movement as the train is started or stopped.

Loose coupling is necessary to enable the train to bend around curves and is an aid

in starting heavy trains, since locomotive power operates on each car in the train

successively and the power is thus utilized to start only one car at a time.

18

To begin with Blue Train. For over five thousand years cotton has been grown on five

different continents, with the first cottons bearing fibers of the length and consistency

suitable for cloth grown in Africa. The plant emerged differently on different continents,

albeit likely some form of ferrying occurred — floating rafts made of coconut debris and

other plant stuff carrying cotton seeds — since the seeds tolerate salt water and retain their

fertility. The first sign that a cotton plant will successfully create the desired white stuff is a

small square. The downy white forms a protective layer around the seeds and clings tenaciously to the plant and must be plucked. When the boll is left to deteriorate on the

stem and be blown about, the seeds are dispersed and new seedlings give birth to future

plants. When ginned, seeds fall to the bottom and can be used for new plants or turned

into cottonseed oil. I learned a lot with him. I learned little things, you know. Little things

mean so much in music, like in everything else, you know? Like the way you build a

house. You get the little things together and then the whole structure will stand up. Monk,

he's always doing something back there that sound so mysterious. He might take a chord, a minor chord and leave the third out. Then he'll say, "This is a minor chord, man," but you don't have a minor third in there, so you don't know what it is. You say, "How do you know it's a minor chord?" "That's what it is, a minor chord with the third out." And when he plays the thing, it'll just be in the right place and voice the right way to have that minor feel. Little things like that, you know.

19

To begin with Acknowledgement. It was a bright golden moment burnished by trumpet

and trombone, offshore brass we were never not aware was there. Beams we thought back

to, streaming down in the redwood chapel, otherwise caught in the leaves or the needles,

apostolic, striated light. Trane's edge cutting right thru. To think was to be fed an affection

for indefiniteness blur fostered. To think was to be in brass territory, no matter one played a

legbone flute. And every now and then, a salt tang, a drift of sea-weed. Rust occurs when

iron comes in contact with moist air. Given sufficient time, oxygen and water, iron will eventually convert entirely to this reddish brittle coating. Steel rusts because it contains

iron, but this rusting can be limited by bluing, rubbing oil into the metal. Just take a cloth

and swipe it over the metallic surface, shoving oil into the hard but minutely pockmarked

steel. Brass technically does not rust, but corrodes, especially when exposed to ocean air

or other salty conditions. Plants do not rust, but decompose. Damage to plants can result

in excessive flowering and seed production, whereby their extinction might be prevented.

Boll-weevil's coming, and the winter's cold. Make cotton stalks look rusty. Drought had caused the soil to take all water from the streams. Dead birds were found in wells a

hundred feet below the ground. Such was the winter when the cotton flower bloomed.

Time and space have no meaning in a canefield. Cane leaves swaying, rusty with talk. The

scent of cane came from the copper pan and drenched the forest and the hill that sloped

to factory town, beneath its fragrance. Once cut sugar cane begins to lose its sugar. Dusk

takes polish from the rails. To squeeze out the last sweetness. Trane's cauterizing cut.

20

To begin with inherence. I sit there and run over chord progressions and sequences, and

eventually, I usually get a song—or songs—out of each little musical problem. After I've

worked it out on the piano, I then develop the song further on tenor, trying to extend it

harmonically. The sea itself was a ship which had crashed, it seemed to suggest, coaxing

an evaporative language and logic from its image of ocean as wrecked, predecessor

desert. The desert too was a ship which had sunk, it went on to announce, etheric debris

or amniotic debris, dessicated crib and crypt rolled into one. Fold upon fold, line upon line and wrinkle upon wrinkle gathered, one moment suggesting the Assyrian god

Humbaba, whose face was built of intestines, and next the Aztec rain god Tlaloc, whose

face consisted of two intertwining snakes. The band, which could only have been the

Crossroads Choir, partook of an elastic, variable aspect equal to if not greater than that of

the audience and the structure (whatever and wherever it was) in which we were gathered.

Their entrance threatened to go on forever—a slow numberless stampede, as if it were of

musician after hyperbolic musician which made me wonder whether the stage could hold them all. It seemed they were every band I'd ever heard of or even dreamt I'd

heard all rolled into one. The whole concept of materialism only applies to very

abstract entities. What I mean by material is anything which has the property of simple

location. When we examine these primary materials of a simplified issue we shall find

that they are in truth only to be justified as being elaborate logical constructions of a

high degree of abstraction. We have mistaken our abstractions for concreted realities.

21

To begin with inherence. I create an inherence through piecing one word or scrap at

a time. Starting with a sentence in the middle and then going to the beginning and the

end of it at the same time, both directions at once. Putting my left and right hand in the

middle of the page and inscribing simultaneously in a mirrored relationship of forward

and backward script. She utilizes both of her hands after an injury to her right hand during

her early childhood. She enjoins that ambidexterity should be observed and encouraged

in her republic. We can utilize the concept, that the realization is a gathering of things into the unity of a prehension; and that what is thereby realized is the prehension,

and not the things. The unity of a prehension defines itself as a *here* and *now,* and the

things so gathered into the grasped unity have essential reference to other places and other

times. Everything is everywhere at all times. For every location involves an aspect of itself

in every other location. Thus every spatio-temporal standpoint mirrors the world. Trane's

voice, strained and stranded, infiltrated hers. Trane woven into it all saying horns don't go

there. The closest he'd come to trying to put what he was after in words was the image of blocks turning into waves—the way cars on a freeway, heard from a distance, tend

to sound like the ocean. Linters, silky fibers which adhere to cotton seeds after ginning,

can be used in the manufacture of paper. I imagined all the life I couldn't see, marmots

in Canada, otters in Alaska.

AFTER

I have utilized multiple internet and print sources in order to create the textures of *Brilliant Corners*, borrowing, riffing, and making. For appropriations that have been taken from wordings of a singular caste, that is, when an individual's mind and hand seems indelibly connected to the words engaged, I credit these in "After . . .". Only occasionally do I quote verbatim. Often I have fudged or budged a word or two, and sometimes I have added whole new phrases and sentences, and reordered the passage. However, all said, I am much beholden to these originators for the following passages:

1.
Simone White, Walter Benjamin, Giorgio Agamben, "Citation . . . origin."
John Milton, "So . . . alone."
Percy Bysshe Shelley, "And thou . . .sea-music."

2.
 Samuel Taylor Coleridge, "O'er . . . Hope."
John Addington Symonds, "Dante . . . ocean role."
Henry David Thoreau, "Does he . . . within him."

3.
Simone White, "The color . . . human being."

4.
Richard Diebenkorn, "I began to feel . . . things right."

5.
Richard Diebenkorn, "I want . . .desire."

6.

Richard Diebenkorn, "I discovered . . . revealing."

7.

Gearaldine Westbrook, "I just . . . my own."

Annie Mae Young, "My daddy . . . dress."

8.

Annie Mae Young," I got . . . level."

Nathaniel Mackey, "Time . . . in it."

9.

Joanna Pettway, "The time . . . quilting."

Marsha Jane Pettway, "I sit . . . all right."

Leola Pettway "Quilts . . . cold"; "I . . . quilt."

Nathaniel Mackey, "I saw . . . opera glass."

10.

Gilles Deleuze, "Inclusion . . . subject."

Joanna Pettway, "Go to . . . in the quilt."

11.

Robert Farris Thompson with Robert Bryant, Fu-Kiau Bunseki, Lydia Cabrera, John M. Janzen, Charley Leland, Wyatt MacGaffey, Karl Laman, Maude Southwell Wahlman, and multiple unnamed Kongolese and their descendants, "Kongo Charms . . . living."

12.

Robert Farris Thompson, Robert Bryant, Fu-Kiau Bunseki, "The Ki-Kongon . . . Won't you come."
Jonathon White, "automobile-size . . . saltiness."
13.
Nathaniel Mackey, "There seems to be . . . desire."
Thelonious Monk, "When you look . . . imagination."

14.
Thelonious Monk, "I get tired . . . laugh at."

15.
Emily Bronte, "I gazed . . . slate."
Nathaniel Mackey, "Thirst . . despair."
Thelonious Monk, "What . . . notes differently."

16.
Thelonious Monk, "Writing about music . . . club."
Robin D. G. Kelley, "Henry Minton . . . standard."
Thelonious Monk, "The important thing . . . mathemeticians."

17.
John Coltrane, "I'd go by . . . down together."

18.
John Coltrane, "I learned. . . you know."

19.
Nathaniel Mackey, "It was a bright . . .legbone flute."

Jean Toomer, "And every . . . sea weed." "Boll-weevil . . . the rails."
Nathaniel Mackey "To squeeze . . . sweetness."

20.
John Coltrane, "I sit there . . . harmonically."
Nathaniel Mackey, "The sea . . . into one."
Alfred North Whitehead, "The whole concept . . . realities."

21.
John Coltrane, "Starting . . . at once."
Alfred North Whitehead, "We can utilize . . . the world."
Nathaniel Mackey, "Trane's voice . . . ocean."

ABOUT THE AUTHOR

Jeanne Heuving is the 2022 Judith E. Wilson Fellow in Poetry at Cambridge University, UK. She is the author of *Transducer* (Chax Press), *Mood Indigo* (selva oscura press), and *Incapacity* (Chiasmus Press); and the editor of *Nathaniel Mackey, Destination Out: Essays On His Work* (U of Iowa Press) and the co-editor along with Tyrone Williams of *Inciting Poetics: Thinking and Writing Poetry* (Recencies Series, University of New Mexico Press). Her monograph *The Transmutation of Love and Avant-Garde Poetics* appears in the Modern and Contemporary Poetics series (U of Alabama Press). Heuving is a professor in the Interdisciplinary Arts and Science program at the University of Washington (UW) Bothell and is on the graduate faculty in the English Department at UW Seattle. She founded the MFA in Creative Writing & Poetics at UW Bothell and served as its first director. She is the recipient of grants from the Fulbright Foundation, National Endowment for the Humanities, Simpson Humanities Center, and the Beinecke Library at Yale (H.D. Fellowship) .

ABOUT CHAX

Chax Press has always sought to bring a sense of expanded possibility to the book, acted out in content, design, typography, materials, and structures. We began in 1984 and have published some 250 books, including artists' books, fine press books, hybrid letterpress-digital books, chapbooks, trade paperback books, and casebound or boxed publications. In 2021 the Chax Press director received the Lord Nose Award (named in honor of the legendary Jonathan Williams of The Jargon Society), conferred by the Community of Literary Magazines and Presses (CLMP), for lifetime achievement in literary publishing.

Chax is a nonprofit 501(c)(3) organization which depends on suppport from various government & private funders, and, primarly, from individual donors and readers. Please join our mission by supporting Chax. You will find us online at *https://chax.org*, and you can email us at *chaxpress@chax.org*.

Correspondence to the press should be sent to
Chax Press / 1517 N Wilmot Rd no. 264 / Tucson AZ 85712 / USA

Type fonts in this book are Albertina MT Pro & Optima
Book & Cover Design by Charles Alexander
Printer & Binder: KC Book Manufacturing